GOT 90 SECONDS?

To
Sonya:
Read to learn –
Learn to think!

Gloria Suridenoki

GOT 90 SECONDS?

QUICK QUOTES & NOTES
TO ENCOURAGE AND INSPIRE

Gloria Swardenski,
Internationally Known Life & Business Coach

iUniverse, Inc.
New York   Lincoln   Shanghai

Got 90 Seconds?
Quick Quotes & Notes to Encourage and Inspire

iUniverse, Inc.

For information address:
iUniverse, Inc.
2021 Pine Lake Road, Suite 100
Lincoln, NE 68512
www.iuniverse.com

ISBN: 0-595-32274-3

Printed in the United States of America

I'd like to dedicate this book to my Mom.
"Tell me that you won't, but don't tell me that you can't!"
Thanks for empowering me.

Acknowledgments:

I'd like to especially thank a very special person whom I lovingly refer to as my web gal, Tracy Dishman with Virtual Arts, Inc. (www.VirtualArtsOnline.com) Her enthusiasm and "can do" attitude really inspire me and make me think much bigger along the virtual, global highway than just the few people I can see on the paved ones.

I'd also like to thank the Star Press of Muncie, IN for giving me the opportunity to write the Coach's Corner for them. They have been just wonderful in supporting me and encouraging me to keep the keyboard keys clicking away.

A big hug is also well deserved for my partner in life and dreams, Todd, and my four beautiful kiddos, Todd, Jr., Nicole, Brett, and Gloria Jean. You give me infinite ideas to write about and clear inspiration on what makes my life most worth living.

Contents

Dear Readers:

Thank you for taking a few minutes and taking a peek at my book!

I'd like to take just a minute and share with you the story of how this book came about. (Maybe you'll find a little inspiration here, too!)

Over a year ago now, I had the idea of doing a newspaper column. At the time, I didn't know what it would be, but I thought it might be fun. I started scanning the newspaper and decided it needed a place for some inspiration. I pictured in my mind what the column would be like, how long it would be, where it would be in the paper, and even saw my picture there. I picked out a name for my then imaginary column, and played with my bi-line. I told everyone that I wanted to be a newspaper columnist! Scary!!

Finally, one day, I decided it was time to make the call. That's right—I made the call! I knew no one at the paper, had no inside connections, and was somewhat of an oddity as a "personal coach." The gentleman at the paper just glibly suggested I send over a few samples.

I sat at my computer and spit out 3 ideas. With the wonder of technology, I sent them over in a simple e-mail format and let it go. A few days later, he e-mailed me back that he liked them and asked for 8—10 more. Once again, I sat down at the keyboard and began writing what I had been talking about for literally months. The next e-mail I received was this: "Yes, we like these and would like to include them in our paper. Do you think you could do these everyday?" Mission accomplished!

Since that time, newspaper subscribers everywhere have stopped me and shared with me how much they enjoy my column. Laura shared that she is a better person for having read my columns. Sue proclaimed that my thoughts helped her through a somewhat messy divorce.

Susan declared she was going to start that new business because of one of my columns that is hanging on her refrigerator. And still many others tell me they have coffee with me every morning as they flip through the morning paper.

After one of my seminars, an elderly lady named Virginia told me that she gets upset when she misses a column because she doesn't get to cut it out. And when I shared with the group that I was thinking of putting them together in a book, they cheered, and I knew it was time. My desire is that you will enjoy this collection as much as these readers already have.

Never underestimate the power of your dream. It may surprise you and actually come true. It has for me!!

Gratefully,

Gloria

How to Use This Book:

When I first started writing my columns, an elderly gentleman invited me to go to lunch with him and his wife. I gladly accepted and felt honored as he was pretty well-known in the community and I had heard about his work.

As we began eating, he asked me a simple question, "What is the purpose of the columns you write?" My answer, "To get people to think." Needless to say, he smiled.

That continues to be my motivation for each column I write, and this, too, is the opportunity available for you in the reading of this book.

There are 100 different Quotes & Notes included here. I would encourage and challenge you over the next 100 days to set aside a few minutes to have coffee or tea with me. Read each page in less than 90 seconds, and then take a minute or two to explore your own thoughts.

What do you think about what you just read? Do you agree with the thought presented or would you like to challenge it? How does the thought make you feel? Is there an action you need to take regarding that thought? Is there someone else you might enjoy sharing this thought with and getting their perspective?

On the bottom of each page, I have included lines for you to write down your own thoughts. Then tuck the book away in your purse, lay it on the coffee table or in the magazine rack in the bathroom and off you go—encouraged, inspired, and thinking!!

"The real purpose of books is to trap the mind into doing its own thinking."
~ Christopher Morley

1

"Making the decision to have a child—it's monumentous. It is to decide forever to have your heart go walking around outside your body."
—Elizabeth Stone

ରେ ରେ ରେ ରେ ରେ ରେ ରେ ରେ ରେ ରେ ରେ

With the dedication of this book to my mother, I'd like to take the opportunity to share a story from my childhood. On one particular school night, I was sitting at the kitchen table trying to do my homework. The assignment that night was to come up with several paragraphs of writing on many different topics. I sat in tears because the ideas just wouldn't come and I cried in desperation, "I can't do this!" My mother, who I felt then was the meanest mother in town, didn't come to my rescue, but rather looked me in the eyes and said, "Tell me that you won't, but don't tell me that you can't!" I had no idea way back then what I would be doing today. Thanks, Mom! Don't rescue your children from responsibility, empower them.

_____

_____

_____

_____

_____

2

"If people concentrated on the really important things in life, there'd be a shortage of fishing poles."
—Doug Larson

CЗCЗCЗCЗCЗCЗCЗCЗCЗCЗCЗ

Maybe you have never been fishing before, but whether you have or not, I'm sure you can get a mental picture of what fishing would be like. You are sitting in the gently swaying boat with the sun just peaking up over the trees. A soft breeze is blowing across your face. You can smell the pine trees. All that you can hear are birds chirping merrily, a few frogs croaking in the distance, and the leaves rustling in the gentle wind. You look around and see the beautiful creation that God has created for you to enjoy. You may even feel a tug on your line. So what are the really important things? Take some time to go fishing even if it's only in your imagination and see for yourself.

_____

_____

_____

_____

_____

3

"To know what is right and not to do it is the worst
cowardice."

—Confucius

෴෴෴෴෴෴෴෴෴෴෴

Have you ever made the conscious choice to do the wrong thing?
You may never have murdered or stolen a thing, but it can be the
little things that catch us off guard. For example, it may have just
seemed easier to tell the teacher that your dog ate your homework
than to accept responsibility for your laziness in not getting it
done. It may have seemed like such a small thing to tell the boss the
project was almost complete when you hadn't even started. Maybe
you chose to say I don't know when you really did. It takes courage
to accept responsibility for our actions when we know that we have
done something wrong. But sometimes it takes even more courage
to do what is right in the first place. Be courageous and do right.

_____

_____

_____

_____

_____

4

"Maturity is reached the day we don't need to be lied to
about anything."
—Frank Yerby

 CB CB CB CB CB CB CB CB CB CB CB

Are you mature enough to handle the truth? Truth sometimes can
sting and hurt even when it comes from the best intentions of
another. Ask any husband if he tells his wife the real truth when she
comes home from the beauty shop and asks if he likes her hair! Or
better yet, when she may ask, "Does this dress make me look fat?"
But beyond that, probably the hardest truth to accept may come in
the form of well-deserved correction. Challenge yourself to take
correction and even uninvited advice with graciousness and an
attitude of learning—even if your dear husband tells you the truth
about that dress. Don't settle for anything less than the truth.

_____

_____

_____

_____

_____

5

"You don't stop laughing because you grow old; you grow old because you stop laughing."
—Michael Pritchard

ଔଔଔଔଔଔଔଔଔଔଔଔ

Have you ever noticed how children have the most pleasant giggles around? Just listening to their giggle can make you giggle. Life for a child is light and easy with very few cares of the world. Maybe children know something about this thing we call laughter that we may have forgotten. Think about it. There is nothing quite like a good, hearty laugh. Something just catches your funny bone and you laugh so hard you start to cry. Then when the moment of laughter passes, you take a deep breath and somehow life just feels lighter. Share a funny story, tell a friend a new joke, tickle a child, or just be silly. Remember what it was like to be young, and laugh today.

_____

_____

_____

_____

_____

6

"We ourselves feel that what we are doing is just a drop in the ocean. But the ocean would be less because of that missing drop."
—Mother Teresa

ෲෲෲෲෲෲෲෲෲෲෲ

Do you ever feel insignificant, small, just a drop in the ocean of humanity? It can feel very overwhelming when you think about all the billions of people in the world. Really, who am I in the sea of so many? The simple answer to that is that you are you. There is no other water droplet anywhere that is just like you, that thinks like you, or even laughs like you. No one else who can contribute to this world quite like you through thought or deed. You are a unique individual with purpose and design. A very special someone who can make a difference. The ocean would be less if you did not exist. Be grateful today for the gift that is you.

_____

_____

_____

_____

_____

7

"Marriage should be a duet—when one sings, the other claps."
—Joe Murray

಄಄಄಄಄಄಄಄಄಄಄

In any relationship, one of the most destructive forces is jealousy. It can show up at work, at home, and on the basketball court. It comes from an attitude that someone else has an advantage over you that you cannot overcome. How can you chase away the green-eyed monster? Begin by celebrating the accomplishments and victories of the other. Congratulate your co-worker on his promotion. Cheer for your husband or wife when they have had a great day. Applaud for your neighbor who just bought that beautiful new car. Then focus on developing your own talents and strengths that will provide the next opportunity for you to succeed. Replace the jealousy with joy for others and yourself.

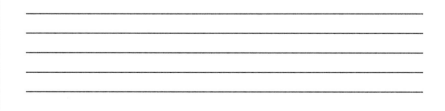

8

"The greatest gift you can give another is the purity of your attention."
—Richard Moss, MD

CBCBCBCBCBCBCBCBCBCBCB

There are so many things that vie for our attention these days. Distractions are everywhere. It can happen at work during a meeting with someone and the phone rings. You try to graciously excuse yourself because of an important call. It can happen at home during a family dinnertime and a telemarketer rings in. You jump up from the table as if a bomb will go off if not answered by the third ring. It can happen on a dinner date with someone special when you are interrupted with friendly faces all beckoning you to come and say hello, causing you to lose track of your conversation. Make it a point today to eliminate the distractions, and give the greatest gift you can give—you.

_____

_____

_____

_____

_____

9

"If most of us are ashamed of shabby clothes and shoddy furniture, let us be more ashamed of shabby ideas and shoddy philosophies."
—Albert Einstein

ぼぼぼぼぼぼぼぼぼぼぼ

When was the last time you had a really good idea? An idea that solved a problem, brought someone joy, or helped relieve some stress. It really is fun to be creative and let the ideas flow, and if you are looking for ways to have even better ideas then here are a few ideas for you. Begin by treasuring your ideas. These ideas could be about anything from how to throw a fantastic party, to your next book idea, or your next business meeting. Write them down in a very special book or create your own idea box so that they will not be lost. Periodically review them and decide if they are something that you would like to pursue now or save for later. Welcome your brilliant ideas and more will follow.

_____

_____

_____

_____

_____

10

"Don't put off for tomorrow what you can do today, because if you enjoy it today you can do it again tomorrow."
—James A Michener

ͼͽͼͽͼͽͼͽͼͽͼͽͼͽ

Here's a new twist on the procrastinator's creed. What is it that you have been putting off that you might really enjoy doing after all? It may be something as simple as cleaning up a pile of papers off your desk. The key is to be creative and create ways that will make the chore much more enjoyable. When it comes to those piles of papers, what would be some ways that you could make them just a little bit more fun to deal with? Maybe buy some color folders, create notes with smiley faces for the next person, or just rearrange those organizational bins for a fresh look. Make everything that you do enjoyable, and when it feels like a drudgery figure out how to lighten it up. Enjoy today so you can look forward to doing it again tomorrow.

_____

_____

_____

_____

_____

11

"Never eat more than you can lift."
—Miss Piggy's Guide to Life

ങ്ങങ്ങങ്ങങ്ങങ്ങ

So, what's on your menu for today? A couple pieces of toast with a
slab of lateness as you run out the door? A big, juicy burger with all
the works and at least 36 extra grams of stress on the side? A
dinner for two with iced tea and lemon slices full of sour thoughts
of the day? Maybe a midnight snack of a bowl of ice cream topped
with the guilt of no time for exercise? Time to change your diet and
take on Miss Piggy's motto. If life is feeling heavy than maybe it's a
great time to learn the art of simply saying no. Say no to the
constant lateness. Say no to the stress. Say no to the eating of
unhealthy foods. Say no to the excuse of no time for exercise. Say
no to the negative thoughts. Just say no.

_____
_____
_____
_____
_____

12

"A truth that's told with bad intent beats all the lies you can invent."
—William Blake

C３C３C３C３C３C３C３C３C３C３C３

Have you ever come across someone who prides himself on speaking his mind? He feels that it is his divine right and even duty to tell the world what he thinks. And what he thinks may be true, but the intent behind that truth can cut like a knife. As a result, a relationship may become estranged and the poor gentleman is left with the question of why since he merely told the truth. What caused the friction? The intention behind the words. Did he really have the best interests of the hearer at heart? Somehow we are created with an innate sense that tells us if this is so. It's almost as if we have invisible antennas that warn us of jealousy, judgment, and misguided intentions. Tell the truth, but always in love.

_____

_____

_____

_____

_____

13

"It's not easy taking my problems one at a time when they refuse to get in line."
—Ashleigh Brilliant

ෆෆෆෆෆෆෆෆෆෆෆ

We've probably all heard the expression "when it rains, it pours" which is a great slogan for Morton's salt, but not very fun when it comes to problems. There's also another saying that problems come in three's, so if you are on number 2—watch out!—number 3 is coming your way. Well, I'd like to challenge that idea and give you just a little insight on how to change the direction on your problem magnet day. I use the word magnet because essentially you are. You attract different things into your life like a magnet attracts metal. So, usually, if someone is attracting negative things then it is time to change the charge on the magnet. How? Begin with your attitude. Positive attitudes attract positive.

_____

_____

_____

_____

_____

14

"Although the world is full of suffering, it is also full of the overcoming of it."
—Helen Keller

જીજીજીજીજીજીજીજીજીજીજી

On the previous page, we began to challenge the idea of you being a problem magnet. Living in such a way that problems and issues arrive at your doorstep unannounced and uninvited too often. We began with changing the charge of this problem magnet by choosing to have a positive attitude. The next step is to look for ways to solve the problem. Not ignore it, sweep it under the rug, or put it off for another day, but truly solve it once and for all. Many problems are often the same kind only because we do not deal with them fully in the first place. There is no problem that is too big to overcome. If Hellen Keller who was both deaf and blind was able to overcome, then so can you. Fully solve today's problems.

_____

_____

_____

_____

_____

15

"The Wright brothers flew right through the smoke screen of impossibility."
—Charles F. Kettering

ɞɷɞɷɞɷɞɷɞɷɞɷ

Can you imagine what it must have been like for the Wright brothers in school? Somewhere along the way they got this crazy idea that man could fly. Maybe they sat in school and drew pictures of men with flaps on their arms, helmets on their heads, and a feather here or there. A teacher or their parents may have told them to throw away those crazy ideas, for after all, if God meant for us to fly He would've given us wings! The neighbors may have wondered what they were up to next as they cut and hammered in their garage. Today, airplanes are a part of everyday life with abundant frequent flyer miles. Look up to the sky and notice the airplanes. See through the smoke screen of impossibility.

_____

_____

_____

_____

_____

16

"Doctors and scientists said that breaking the four-minute mile was impossible, that one would die in the attempt. Thus, when I got up from the track after collapsing at the finish line, I figured I must be dead."
—Roger Bannister

෬෬෬෬෬෬෬෬෬෬෬෬

On May 6, 1954, Roger Bannister, a 25 year old from Harrow on the Hill, England, did the impossible. He broke the record that no one believed could ever be broken. He ran a mile in 3:59.4. What was so extra special about Roger? Nothing really. He was made out of the same stuff as the rest of us, but he had an insatiable desire to win. He trained hard when he didn't really feel like it. He watched his mental strength and guarded it. He had his eyes fixed on the prize and never let it go. And today, what was once the impossible is now the expected. So, what is the goal that feels like the impossible for you? Determine to do the impossible.

_____

_____

_____

_____

_____

17

"God gave you a gift of 86,400 seconds today. Have you used one to say 'thank you'?"

—William Arthur Ward

Let's change the calendar a little bit and make today a day of thanksgiving. Let today be a day to say thank you to God who has given us life, health, and a place to lay our heads at night in peace. Let's say thank you to our family for their unconditional love and support. Let's be grateful for our friends who know us as we are and yet continue to be our friends anyway. Let's be grateful to those we don't know, but take the time to greet us with a smile anyway. How can you express your gratitude today? A prayer, a note, flowers, an e-mail, a telephone call, a smile? It only takes a few seconds to say thank you, but it is never time that is wasted. To all of my readers and supporters near and far, I say thank you! Be thankful today.

_____

_____

_____

_____

_____

18

"What we usually pray to God is not that His will be done,
but that He approve ours."
—Helga Bergold Gross

CBCBCBCBCBCBCBCBCBCBCB

How often have you gone to God in prayer with a wish list of
things that you were asking for? God became a Santa Claus for all
the things that we wanted or didn't want in our lives. There are
many aspects of prayer and even Jesus himself prayed for his daily
bread, but in the end he asked that God's will be done. What if
instead of asking for the usual list, you simply asked for God's will
to be done in sickness and in health, for richer or for poorer, in the
good times and the bad? It is a simple letting go process of all the
things you think are most important and letting God direct your
steps. It is a path of trusting, simple as it may seem. May God's will
be done in your life today.

_____

_____

_____

_____

_____

19

"One of the greatest sources of energy is pride in what you are doing."
—Spokes

દ્યદ્યદ્યદ્યદ્યદ્યદ્યદ્યદ્યદ્ય

What are you doing? Are you proud of it? There are many things that we do in life, and no matter how simple or mundane or boring it is, we should do it in a way that we can always be proud of our efforts. Are you proud of the way you handle your responsibilities and projects at work? Are you proud of the way you hug your wife and kids with love and admiration for who they are? Are you proud of the way you handle your finances by having a plan for the future and not overspending? Are you proud of the way you drive with respect and kindness for other drivers? If you are coming home at the end of the day tired and spent, then take a look at what you are doing. Be proud of all that you do.

_____

_____

_____

_____

_____

20

"Forgiving and being forgiven are two names for the same thing. The important thing is that a discord has been resolved."
—C. S. Lewis

છ૪છ૪છ૪છ૪છ૪છ૪છ૪છ૪છ૪છ૪

Is there a discord in your life that needs to be resolved? Not just shoved under the rug, ignored, and slowly forgotten about, but fully resolved. If you are looking for an inner peacefulness then this is the place to start. There is nothing more unpeaceful than harboring bitterness, resentment, and anger toward another person or situation. How can you do this? Begin by stepping out of denial and accepting what is. Look at the truth of what is and do not resist or try to fight it. Then take responsibility for yourself and yourself only. You have no control over how others act or react, but you do have complete control over your own attitudes and actions. Resolve any discord with forgiveness and live peacefully.

_____

_____

_____

_____

_____

21

"People in distress will sometimes prefer a problem that is familiar to a solution that is not."
—Neil Postman

෪෪෪෪෪෪෪෪෪෪෪෪

Do you ever wonder why a person in an abusive situation stays there? Do you ever wonder why a person who hates his job stays there for years and years? People who are in distress, who are suffering, will often stay within those situations because those situations are normal or familiar. It is all they know. As uncomfortable as it seems to an outsider, the unknown and even sometimes the solution is much more uncomfortable simply because they are afraid. In what areas of your life are you suffering? Are you afraid of the solution because it feels that you may be asking for too much and it just feels wrong somehow? Make today the day to stop the suffering by stepping into the fear of the solution.

_____

_____

_____

_____

_____

22

"When people go to work they shouldn't have to leave their hearts at home."
—Betty Bender

ରେ ରେ ରେ ରେ ରେ ରେ ରେ ରେ ରେ ରେ

Along with your briefcase, handbags, and boxed lunch, remember to take your heart with you to work today. It is so easy to kiss our spouses good-bye, walk out the front door, and put on the emotionless game face of our working lives. Decide to make today different by actually taking your heart to work. Take along the heart of passion that you may have had when you first stepped onto the job; the heart of pride that derives great satisfaction in productivity, efficiency, and a job well done; the heart of compassion for those with whom you work instead of backbiting and criticism; and the heart of service for your customers as you treat them with respect and thankfulness for their business. Heart—don't leave home without it.

_____

_____

_____

_____

_____

23

"If you don't want anyone to know, don't do it."
—Chinese Proverb

಍಍಍಍಍಍಍಍಍಍಍

Have you ever done anything that you absolutely, positively hoped
that no one would ever find out about? I think we all have at one
time or another, and except for a tiny few, most of the hidden
things probably were found out in the end. Depending on how
long the secret was kept hidden, it may have actually felt like a huge
relief that the truth was finally made known and you were free
from the bondage that comes from keeping secrets. It is a much
freer way to live to ask yourself the question—Would I not want
anyone to know that I did this? Would I be embarrassed if my
parents/children/boss/pastor found out that I did this? Live a life
that is free from the bondage of secrets.

_____
_____
_____
_____
_____

24

"Without libraries what have we?
We have no past and no future."
—Ray Bradbury

ෙෙෙෙෙෙෙෙෙෙෙ

When was the last time you took a trip to the library? You might
think this is a strange question, but one to think about nonetheless.
Libraries are full of books, magazines, and other resources that help
us discover our past, learn from it, and teach it to our children. It is
an endless supply of how-to information that not only gives us
guidance, but helps us learn from the mistakes and wisdom of
others. We can fill our minds with autobiographies of positive,
successful people who inspire us to dream and reach for more than
we ever thought we could. We can learn about starting our own
business, financial planning, child rearing, and even foreign
language studies. Learn from the past and invest in the future. Plan
some time to visit the library.

_____

_____

_____

_____

_____

25

"The time to relax is when you don't have time for it."
—Sydney J. Harris

ↃↄↃↄↃↄↃↄↃↄↃↄↃↄↃↄ

Have you ever had a problem that you spent hours and hours trying to solve, then finally gave up, only to come back to it the next day and solve it within minutes? What happened? Our brains have become so full and so fixed on the problem that the solution evades us. You may be facing a deadline or for many accountants, April 15th, but when you cannot see the solution, the solution may be to take the time to relax. Leave the office, take a nice hot shower or bath, browse through your favorite magazine, or go for a walk. Your brain is an amazing creation that is full of surprises. Give your mind the time and space to allow the solution to rise to the top. Relax.

_____

_____

_____

_____

_____

26

"You can get through life with bad manners, but it's easier with good manners."

—Lillian Gish

ରେ ରେ ରେ ରେ ରେ ରେ ରେ ରେ ରେ ରେ

Here's a very simple tip for making your life a little bit easier today. Think about it—how easy would life be if everyone you knew had and actually put into practice good manners? You were greeted with a smile and a hello everywhere you went. You actually enjoyed driving because people watched out for one another and let you in their lane when you needed. You were free to take your time because there wasn't a rush to be first. In this busy, stand-up-for-yourself society, we sometimes feel that the nice guy always finishes last, so we give up a piece of our goodness that is demonstrated in good manners. Stand up for yourself, your goals, and your dreams, but do it the easy way—with good manners.

_____

_____

_____

_____

_____

27

"We have to learn to be our own best friends because we fall too easily into the trap of being our worst enemies."
—Roderick Thorp

cececececececececece

Do you ever feel like you are your own worst enemy? You start in on something or come up with a great idea that you think is just such a good thing only to procrastinate or do something that is in your own opinion just plain stupid. You look in the mirror and wonder how you made it through life even this far. It is so easy to fall into this trap of self-loathing and self-criticism. If we were anyone else, we would be much more understanding, forgiving, and encouraging, but we expect so much more from ourselves. Let go of the perfect person you think you should be, and accept the person that you are right now. Best friends accept the flaws and love anyway. Be your own best friend.

_____

_____

_____

_____

_____

28

"Love thy neighbor as thyself."
—Matthew 19:19

CRCRCRCRCRCRCRCRCRCR

There's something missing in our society today that most may believe is a good thing. It is something that many believe we are just born with, and it is a bad thing that needs to be done away with. While there is a dark side to this concept, there is also a very positive and healthy upside. For I have seen that without it, we are faced with divorce, contention, and divisions. With it, we become an attractive person and begin attracting positive things into our lives. What am I referring to? I am talking about loving ourselves enough to be selfish. Now after you finish gasping, understand that the selfishness to which I am referring is not at the expense of another. Intrigued? Begin the journey to discover what it means to love thyself through a healthy selfishness.

_____

_____

_____

_____

_____

29

"The better we feel about ourselves, the fewer times we have to knock somebody else down to feel tall."

—Odetta

CJCJCJCJCJCJCJCJCJCJCJ

Have you ever been really, really hungry? Not necessarily starving, but just really hungry? What is on your mind? Are you interested in world peace, talking about how your day was with your wife, playing a game with your kids, or reading the newspaper? No, you are hungry and all you are thinking about is food! You would do anything to get it including running someone over, taking the last piece, and licking the plate clean. You have a need and you would do anything to have that need met. This is what happens when people have needs that are not getting met. Other people get run over, ignored, lashed out at. Be selfish enough to discover what your needs are.

_____

_____

_____

_____

_____

30

"One of the oldest human needs is having someone to wonder where you are when you don't come home at night."
—Margaret Mead

ભજભજભજભજભજભજભજભજ

The need to be cared for and loved is only a few of the dozens and dozens of needs that we as humans have. As we grow and mature the responsibility for getting those needs met becomes our own through first knowing what we need and communicating effectively to those who can meet that need. For example, a wife may have a need to be cherished. The husband does love his wife, but the wife is still unhappy. Whose responsibility is it for getting the need met? It is easy for the wife to say her husband should try harder or maybe read some self-help books, but ultimately it is the wife's responsibility to simply communicate what she needs. Be selfish enough to learn how to communicate what your needs are.

_____

_____

_____

_____

_____

31

"A lot of what passes for depression these days is nothing more than a body saying that it needs work."
—Geoffrey Norman

ଔଔଔଔଔଔଔଔଔଔଔ

As we live and breathe and grow, our bodies require a lot of work. Our bodies need food, water, exercise, fresh air, clothes, and cleanliness just to name a few. As we continue to uncover what is a healthy selfishness, we must not overlook taking care of the body that has been given to us to dwell in and enjoy for the rest of our lives. An unhealthy body represents an unhealthy attitude and lifestyle. The vehicle, the temple, which has been given to us to serve others, is our body. If our body is out of shape, addicted to drugs or alcohol, sleep-deprived, or abused in any way, we are not physically capable of being our best or serving anyone else. Be selfish enough to take care of your body well.

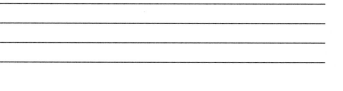

32

"The mind is its own place, and in itself can make a heaven
of hell, a hell of heaven."
—John Milton

ଔଔଔଔଔଔଔଔଔଔଔ

It has been said that the only thing we truly have control over is
our minds, and controlling our minds demands that we have and
practice a healthy selfishness. The Bible tells us specifically that
whatsoever is good, pure, true, honest, of good report, virtuous,
praiseworthy, we should think on these things. Are you filling it
with these things or just the opposite? Having a healthy and vibrant
mind requires that we guard our minds. It is okay to be selfish and
leave a room where there is gossip, profanity, or any negative talk. It
is okay to change the TV channel when ugliness is exploited and
even encouraged. Be selfish enough to explore your own beliefs,
think through your own opinions, and control your own mind.

_____

_____

_____

_____

_____

33

"The miracle is this—the more we share, the more we have."
—Leonard Nimoy

છ્ય છ્ય છ્ય છ્ય છ્ય છ્ય છ્ય

What do you normally think of when you think of someone who is selfish? You may picture someone who has, but does not give like a hungry person refusing to share his food with someone else in need. This type of unhealthy selfishness comes from a place of scarcity or not enough. He may feel that he cannot afford to share. When you come from a place of responsible selfishness, you have the ability to share because you understand that there is plenty to give. You have taken care of your body, so there is no scarcity of energy. You have your needs met, so you need nothing from this person. You have filled your mind with healthy thoughts, so you can share ideas and inspiration. Be selfish and begin to share the abundance that is you.

_____
_____
_____
_____
_____

34

"Yesterday is a canceled check; tomorrow is a promissory note;
today is the only cash you have—so spend it wisely."

—Kay Lyons

છ૪છ૪છ૪છ૪છ૪છ૪છ૪

How are you planning on spending your day today? Are you planning
to spend it enjoying all that life has to offer right now or are you
trying to reclaim lost time from the past? Are you thinking about the
achievements and promises of today or borrowing some hope or
worry from what tomorrow might bring? If you truly want to gain
the joy of living in the present then follow along this path. Begin with
accepting the past and give up any hope of recreating a new one. You
cannot relive it, do it over, take it back, or make it any better. Let go of
the future as well. Surrender your future to God who is the only one
who truly knows what will happen tomorrow. Spend today wisely.

_____
_____
_____
_____
_____

35

"Opportunities are often things you haven't noticed the first time around."
—Catherine Deneuve

೫೫೫೫೫೫೫೫೫೫೫೫

It is astounding when you think about how many opportunities may have come and gone in our lives. Endless opportunities to love, to learn, to achieve. Why do we miss some? It may be that we reacted to a situation or event instead of responding. When you react to something, you instinctively make a quick assessment of what is going on based on a past experience, and try to act in a way that worked well before, or wish you had done before in a similar situation. When you are responding, you are making a conscious choice. You take the time to ask yourself what is really going on, what is happening, am I missing something. See the opportunity by choosing to respond well.

_____

_____

_____

_____

_____

_____

36

"It is not the man who has too little who is poor, but the one who craves more."
—Seneca

ↃↄↃↄↃↄↃↄↃↄↃↄↃↄ

Do you know how to start curbing those cravings? Have more than enough. Yes, build a super-reserve of the things that you need so that you really don't have to spend the time or energy trying to figure out how to get that need met. Make it really simple and begin with the tangible things that are common needs. Begin to stockpile toilet paper, shampoo, soap, deodorant, tissues, and canned goods. It feels good to know that you won't run out for a long, long time. From there you can stop thinking about these necessities and move on to the next level of reserve, maybe money or health. When you create a reserve in one area, the energy and focus naturally flows into other areas. Begin building super-reserves.

_____

_____

_____

_____

_____

37

"Only a fool thinks price and value are the same."
—Antonio Machado

CষCষCষCষCষCষCষCষCষCষCষ

What makes something of value? The concept of value is really based on perception for as the saying goes—One man's trash is another man's treasure. To one it is junk, to the other it has value. Price doesn't matter. By learning what value is and how to add value to everything you do, whether personally or professionally, brings much satisfaction and joy. Adding value is most of the time something that is intangible. It cannot be bought. Adding value simply means finding out what the other person needs and wants, be it a family member or customer, and then doing it. It could be as simple as returning a phone call, following-up, knowledgeable conversation, or service with a smile. Add value to someone else's life and you'll find that you add value to your own.

_____

_____

_____

_____

_____

38

"A life isn't significant except for its impact on other lives."
—Jackie Robinson

છ છ છ છ છ છ છ છ છ છ છ છ

Have you ever thought about the impact that you have on others' lives? It can be a scary thought to think that what we do and say affects other people, but if you want to have a significant life then you will want to profoundly affect other people in a positive way. Over the next couple of pages, let's explore who has had a profound impact on your life and how you can also have a profound impact on others. To begin, think of at least 3 people in your life who have made a life-changing difference. It could be a high school basketball coach, your Mom or Dad, Oprah, or even a stranger. What did this person do or say that affected you? How did it change your life? Be grateful for these significant people.

_____

_____

_____

_____

_____

39

"Somewhere out there is a unique place for you to help others—a unique life role for you to fill that only you can fill."
—Thomas Kinkade

C8C8C8C8C8C8C8C8C8C8C8

We all have a role to fill in this life, and we all have the opportunity to affect others in a profound way. Whether we choose to do so positively or not is up to us. On the previous page, we took a minute to think about a few people who have had a big impact in our lives, those who have truly made a difference. If you feel that you are ready for this challenge of being a positive influence, then the most important thing to remember is to always be your genuine, authentic self. There is no room for pretense, hidden agendas, or ulterior motives here. Be honest, real, true to your values and character, while honoring God, yourself, and others. You communicate as much if not more to the world by who you are than what you do and say. Make a profound impact by being genuine.

_____

_____

_____

_____

_____

40

"To 'coin a phrase' is to place some value on it."
—E. H. Evenson

CRCRCRCRCRCRCRCRCRCRCR

Have you ever had something that you wanted to express but could not find the right words? How did it make you feel when someone else stepped in, caught what you were trying to say, and put it into a few words that had value and meaning. You may have even shouted, "Yes, that's it!" Many times, if someone has profoundly affected you, it was through something that they said. The words that they used were the precise words needed to describe the situation, how they felt about something, or the message they wanted to share. Words can show that we have caught something that may have been as illusive as an idea and make it concrete and real. Words are a gift of a great value. Learn a new word today.

_____

_____

_____

_____

_____

41

"More important than a work of art itself is what it will sow. Art can die, a painting can disappear. What counts is the seed."

—Joan Miro

ജ്ഞ്ജ്ഞ്ജ്ഞ്ജ്ഞ്ജ്ഞ്ജ്ഞ

Have you ever seen a painting or a picture that just stirred something within you and stayed with you? In some magical way, the image was able to plant a seed within you that brought out an emotion that maybe you had never given much thought to before. As we celebrate the arrival of spring each year, we often take the time to think about planting seeds of all different kinds—flower, vegetable, grass seeds. Yet, have you ever given any thought to the seeds you may be planting in the thoughts and lives of others? What will people be thinking and feeling after they have spent some time with you? Will you have planted seeds that help them grow, build confidence, and blossom? Plant seeds of beauty wherever you go.

_____

_____

_____

_____

_____

42

"The chains of habit are generally too small to be felt until
they are too strong to be broken."
—Samuel Johnson

ଔଔଔଔଔଔଔଔଔଔଔଔ

People are such creatures of habit. Day after day we do the same
things over and over not necessarily because we want to, or because
we feel that it adds pleasure or value to our lives, but simply because it
has become a habit. Some are good habits, while others are not. What
are some of your habits? Would you classify these habits as good,
meaning they enhance and enrich your life, or bad, they rob you of
your health, happiness, and well being? Pick one negative habit today
that you would like to really focus on for the next week. Gather any
support you need around you to give you the encouragement and
strength to break those chains. Refuse to be a slave to your bad habits.

_____

_____

_____

_____

_____

43

"The most important things in life aren't things."
—Anonymous

ଔଔଔଔଔଔଔଔଔଔଔ

What do you think is the difference between having a life and having a lifestyle? Maybe you have never really thought much about it before, but there is a big difference. Over the next few pages, I'd like to explore the differences and challenge you to evaluate if you are living a life or just a lifestyle. To begin, let me give you a basic idea of the difference. A lifestyle is about external things—brand name clothes, a beautiful home, a prestigious car, and hanging around with just the right people. Having a life, on the other hand, is to know what matters most to you and you only. Your own priorities and goals determine what you wear, what you drive, and who your closest friends are. Which are you choosing—a life or a lifestyle?

_____

_____

_____

_____

_____

44

"You only live once. But if you work it right, once is enough."
—Fred Allen

CBCBCBCBCBCBCBCBCBCB

On the previous page, we began to take a deeper look into the differences between having a life vs. merely having a lifestyle. Here, I'd like to dive a little deeper into what a lifestyle costs. Having a lifestyle is mostly about things and having an external sense of feeling good about yourself. If you work at the right place, have the right kind of job, drive the right car, and married someone who may be a prized trophy, you may be accepted by society at large. You're popular, accepted, and even looked up to. The cost—your self-esteem, values, and ideals are all at the mercy of everyone around you. When all the commercials change so must you or you become outdated and not taken seriously. Count the cost of your lifestyle.

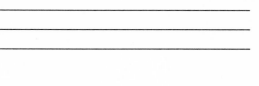

45

"There is more to life than increasing its speed."
—Gandhi

ରେରେରେରେରେରେରେରେରେରେ

As we continue on with the topic of life vs. lifestyle, on the previous page we discussed what a lifestyle costs. Living a shallow lifestyle will cost you your self-esteem and values. It will also drain your energy because it is based on what you cannot control—the opinion of others. In sharp contrast to having an empty lifestyle is having a satisfying and simple life. In life, your self-esteem comes from within you and does not depend on whether you are driving a Lexus or a paid-off Chevy van. Living a life of meaning and substance comes from doing the work that you were meant to do, be it a stockbroker or a garbage man. Life is simple and yet profound because you make conscious choices based on what is most important to you. Live a life of your own choosing.

46

"Enjoy the little things, for one day you may look back and realize they were the big things."
—Robert Brault

CB CB CB CB CB CB CB CB CB CB CB

Are you ready to make the choice to live a satisfying and full life instead of having just a fancy, expensive lifestyle? It takes courage and daring to make this choice, so when you're tired of the rat race here's what is next. Take the time to purposefully design your own ideal life. Write it down. How would it be different from the lifestyle you are living right now? What would need to be included in your life that you don't seem to have time for? What would you need to let go of? Get rid of all the lifestyle trappings that are draining your energy and your wallet. Begin to make the conscious decision to spend your money on what serves you best, not what feeds your image. Design your life so that everything in it has meaning.

_____

_____

_____

_____

_____

47

"Now and then it is good to pause in our pursuit of happiness and just be happy."
—Quoted in The Cockle Bur

જીજીજીજીજીજીજીજીજીજી

Designing your life instead of just living a lifestyle may seem like a daunting task. After all, how can you just walk away from everything that is expected of you? Actually, you aren't walking away, but rather changing the way you look at things. For example, you begin to do things not because they are expected of you, but because you want to. You decide to trade in the expensive Lexus that is driving you away from your family so that you can take a long-awaited family vacation instead. You work hard on a new advertising campaign not because you have an image to protect, but because you want to perform to the best of your abilities and that brings you joy. Do everything today just for the joy of it.

_____

_____

_____

_____

_____

48

"Another flaw in the human character is that everybody
wants to build and nobody wants to do maintenance."
—Kurt Vonnegut

ⓒⓢⓒⓢⓒⓢⓒⓢⓒⓢⓒⓢⓒⓢⓒⓢⓒⓢⓒⓢⓒⓢ

If you are ready to redesign your life, then it is not a matter of
simply building a new one from the ground up, but cleaning up and
maintaining the one that you already have. The cleaning up process
begins by getting rid of the things that just bug the life out of you.
But I warn you, this is not an easy process. If you look at all the
things in life that cause friction, they actually generate energy. If we
didn't have anything to worry about, what would we think about? If
we stopped complaining and started solving what ailed us, we'd
have nothing to talk about. Life would be boring! The truth—these
types of friction are actually causing us grief, holding us back, and
wasting our time and energy. Clean up what is bugging you.

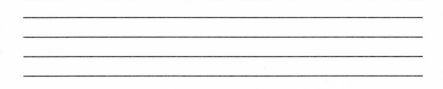

49

"The difference between a hero and a coward is one step sideways."
—Gene Hackman

છ્ય છ્ય છ્ય છ્ય છ્ય છ્ય છ્ય છ્ય

Can you hear it? The whistling in the background as you step out onto the dusty street. Can you see it? The opponent, the obstacle, standing in the way of your dreams. You take a minute to remember. For you've been here before and failed with a near-fatal wound to your spirit. You hear the whistle begin again. You've had some time to heal and decide if you would try again to defeat the bully that is stealing the joy out of your life. Now, the time has come. This time you're a little smarter, a little faster, and a little wiser. You understand that putting up with this bully is not good for anyone. You're ready to stop complaining and take any necessary action. You're ready to put action behind the dream. It's your turn to be a hero.

_____

_____

_____

_____

_____

50

"The hardest thing to learn in life is which bridge to cross
and which to burn."
—Laurence J. Peter

❧❧❧❧❧❧❧❧❧❧❧

We build lots of different bridges in our lives. Some are good and
help us get to where we would like to go with much less time and
effort. Others are not and let in the enemy or wild animals
unaware. As we go through life, we have some tough decisions to
make. We must decide which bridges serve us and which no longer
do. It can be a scary thing though to burn a bridge and never look
back, but when that bridge becomes dangerous or harmful it is
time to let it go. Burn any bridge that keeps you tied to a lifestyle
you no longer want. Burn any bridge that keeps you bound to a
habit that returns at will. Burn the bridge to any person who tears
down the walls of your dream. Burn some bridges today.

_____

_____

_____

_____

_____

51

"A trip to nostalgia now and then is good for the spirit,
as long as you don't set up housekeeping."
—Dan Bartolovic

ભ ભ ભ ભ ભ ભ ભ ભ ભ ભ ભ

What does it mean to get clear of your past? To get clear means that
there is nothing left unresolved. Unresolved issues are like a glass
with cracks in it. No matter how hard you try to fill the glass with
the most pleasant refreshment you can think of, it will continually
drain out and leave you feeling unsatisfied and thirsty. These past
issues could be a dishonest action that you committed against your
integrity and was never made right. It could be you are still
harboring bitterness over a negative comment received or never
apologized for something you may have said. Or it could be that
you are continuing to let someone step over your boundaries to the
point of hurting you. You will never have a full and satisfying life if
you leave things unresolved. Learn how to resolve the unresolved.

_____

_____

_____

_____

_____

52

"A conscience, like a buzzing bee, can make a fellow uneasy
without ever stinging him."
—American Farm & Home Almanac

CBCBCBCBCBCBCBCBCBCBCB

What things from your past have been buzzing around in your
conscience like an annoying bee that just won't go away? Is there a
way to handle this buzzing bee? I'd like to share with you two steps
to solve things fully so you can be clear of your past. The first step
is always communication. Maybe you need to inform another that
what they said or did left you uneasy or maybe you need to say that
you are sorry. Describe what you thought you heard and how it
made you feel. Clarify what happened from your point of view and
ask what did they mean or simply ask why. Make a direct request
that it not happen again and give instructions for the future so it
won't happen again. Resolve past issues with great communication.

_____

_____

_____

_____

_____

53

"Live so your friends can defend you but never have to."
—Arnold H. Glasow

ෆිෆිෆිෆිෆිෆිෆිෆිෆිෆිෆි

To live a life that is clear of the past means leaving nothing unresolved. It means there is nothing left on your conscience that is bugging you that you haven't fully communicated. And while communication is the first step to resolving the past, we do not want to forget to put some action behind the words. Words are wonderful, but the actions that follow are where the power lies. If you borrowed something from your neighbor 3 years ago, return it with a conversation and not just a note. If you did something that you wish you hadn't, give a flower, a book, some token that you care about the person and not just the event. If you damaged something, replace it or restore it to better than new. Keep your friends. Resolve any outstanding debts through action.

_____
_____
_____
_____
_____

54

"My life is in the hands of any fool who makes me lose my temper."
—Joseph Hunter

CBCBCBCBCBCBCBCBCBCBCB

What is it that makes us lose our temper? That makes us so angry that we say things we don't really mean or break things that we wish we hadn't. In my house growing up, I always knew my mother was angry when the metal kitchen cabinets were slammed more times that there were doors. Whenever we would hear it, we as kids knew it was not a good idea to get into Mom's space. And this is the first skill in dealing with anger. When you are feeling angry about something, be sure to give yourself plenty of space. Excuse yourself from the situation and give yourself the gift of thinking it through. Examine why it angered you so. What is really at the source? Give lots of space to your anger.

55

"Anger is a symptom, a way of cloaking and expressing feelings too awful to experience directly—hurt, bitterness, grief and most of all, fear."

—Joan Rivers

೮೩೮೩೮೩೮೩೮೩೮೩೮೩೮೩೮೩೮೩

From the quote above, we can understand anger that is a result of a hurt, bitterness, or grief. It is no fun when someone lies about us. It hurts and makes us angry. It is unjust that a person is abused by a spouse or a parent. It causes us grief and anger, and rightly so. But have you ever thought about being angry simply out of fear? Maybe you are angry because you fear the unknown and have no control over it. Maybe you are afraid of a rejection so you cover it with an angry attitude as if it doesn't matter. Maybe you are afraid of being different so you settle in and remain angry with yourself that you do not have the courage to step out. Do you have a fear that is disguised as anger?

———————————————————————
———————————————————————
———————————————————————
———————————————————————
———————————————————————

56

"Anyone can become angry. That is easy. But to be angry with the right person, to the right degree, at the right time, for the right purpose and in the right way—that is not easy."

—Aristotle

C3CBCBCBCBCBCBCBCBCBCB

Everyone gets angry from time to time. It is a natural emotion that we are created with that is neither good nor bad, but just is. The problem with anger comes from letting it control us to the point of losing control of ourselves. The cause of the anger is up to you to determine with time and consideration, but the next step is to take appropriate action. The goal is to be angry first with the right person. It serves no one to kick the dog! Then to the right degree. Are you overreacting or being too complacent? Then at the right time. You might even ask—is this a good time? Then for the right purpose. Do you want to resolve the issue or just be right? And in the right way. It's okay to be angry, but never to let that anger get the best of you.

_____

_____

_____

_____

_____

57

"If a small thing has the power to make you angry, does that not indicate something about your size?"
—Sydney J. Harris

☙☙☙☙☙☙☙☙☙☙☙

As we have been talking about anger over these last few pages, it would serve us well to take a minute to think about how often we actually do get angry. Is it a rare occasion or a daily habit? If you feel angry more times than not, maybe it is time to challenge what is really happening. Is there an unresolved issue that you are refusing to deal with? Is there a fear that has yet to be challenged? Is there an action that needs to be followed through on? Or all of the above? If the anger you are feeling is showing up too often and holding you bound and confused then it may be time to reach out for help. There are many more colors in the rainbow than red. Be bigger than your anger.

_____

_____

_____

_____

_____

58

"Gossip needn't be false to be evil—there's a lot of truth that shouldn't be passed around."
—Frank A. Clark

ନ୍ଧ ନ୍ଧ ନ୍ଧ ନ୍ଧ ନ୍ଧ ନ୍ଧ ନ୍ଧ ନ୍ଧ ନ୍ଧ ନ୍ଧ ନ୍ଧ

Are you a gossip? I can see readers everywhere gasping in horror at the thought of it. Me, a gossip—I don't think so! We can probably think of someone else who might fit the bill, but never ourselves. Well, even if you have never started a negative rumor or spread a vicious lie, there is a lot of truth to the quote above that gives us some food for thought. Gossip does not have to be a lie to hurt. Sometimes the most hurt is done by spreading a truth that is none of our business to share. Private family matters, grades, confidences, and dreams are just of few of the private things that should remain private. Ask yourself—If it were me would I want others to be talking about it? If not, then don't.

_____

_____

_____

_____

_____

59

"Laziness has many disguises. Soon 'winter doldrums' will
become 'spring fever'."
—Bern Williams

CKCKCKCKCKCKCKCKCKCKCK

As winter is finally giving way to spring, it is time to get ourselves
out of our caves and back into life. No matter what time of year,
there can be no room for laziness. What will laziness look like for
you? It could be that you haven't looked at your goals for awhile, or
maybe you have and are just frustrated or bored with them. Why
not set some fresh goals for yourself for the next 90 days. Did you
know that in the next 90 days you could pay off a credit card, lose
10 pounds, begin an exercise program, set up a budget, plan a
vacation (and actually go!), read 2 books, write a book, plant a
garden, paint a room, start an investment plan, or finish school in
style? What goals would you like to reach in the next 90 days?

_____

_____

_____

_____

_____

60

"No one ever excused himself to success."
—Dave Del Dotto

ભારતભારતભારતભારતભારત

Excuses. Excuses. Excuses! Don't you ever get tired of all the excuses? There are excuses for just about everything. There is the well-known student's excuse of, "the dog ate my homework." The late worker's excuse of, "I set the alarm on PM instead of AM." The senior moment excuse of, "I forgot." The hangover excuse of, "I'm not feeling well." And the lazy man's excuse of, "I didn't have time." Excuses are nothing more than neglecting to take responsibility for your own thoughts and actions. The consequences are limiting beliefs in yourself and your abilities. What is your excuse? What are you saying that is holding you back from being successful with your goals and ambitions? Successful people do not make excuses.

_____

_____

_____

_____

_____

61

"You must get involved to have an impact. No one is impressed with the won-lost record of the referee."
—John H. Holcomb

 C3C3C3C3C3C3C3C3C3C3C3

I think it is a little unfair to say that a referee doesn't have an impact on a game. They do. I have seen football games and basketball games where a call made by the referee decided the outcome of a game. But, at the same time, the referee is not really a player in the game. They are supposed to be impartial observers who are emotionally unattached to the outcome so while they do not mourn a loss, neither do they share in the joy of a win. In the end, nobody congratulates the referee for a job well done. He doesn't walk away with a trophy to celebrate his hard work and efforts in the game. So, in this game called life which are you? Are you an impartial observer who cares little about the outcome or a player who goes for the win? Be a player.

_____

_____

_____

_____

_____

62

"God gives every bird his worm, but he does not throw it
into the nest."
—Swedish Proverb

ભારત ભારત ભારત ભારત ભારત ભારત

A few years ago, I gave my husband a bird feeder for Father's Day. I
cannot say that I have ever been an avid fan of bird watching, but
since this feeder is hanging in the tree in our backyard, it has been fun
to see all the different birds that have found this free food. But as I
watch them and think about this free food and how easy it must be
for them, I am reminded that they really are not much different from
us. They have to build their nests and find just the perfect tree to raise
their families in. They have to brave the storms and outsmart the
predators. They have to get up in the morning to beat the early bird
rush and earn their living for the day. Is there free food out there for
you? I bet there is, but you might have to do some work to get it.

_____

_____

_____

_____

_____

63

"It is wise to remember that you are one of those who can be fooled some of the time."
—Laurence J. Peter

೫೫೫೫೫೫೫೫೫೫೫

When was the last time someone pulled the wool over your eyes? It could've been a friend who was playing a joke. It could've been a phone call from a telemarketer telling you that you just won a fantastic trip to Florida for free. Or it could've been a small child with big blue eyes and long eyelashes pleading ignorance about the missing cookies. It is wise to remember that we all can be fooled some of the time because it reminds us who we are and how much life has taught us. We learn by doing, seeing, believing and sometimes we are wrong. We are human beings who make mistakes and misjudgments. Don't be so foolish as to judge another too harshly for his foolishness. Next time, it may be you.

_____

_____

_____

_____

_____

64

"It's a funny thing about life; if you refuse to accept anything
but the best, you very often get it."
—W. Somerset Maugham

ଔଔଔଔଔଔଔଔଔଔଔ

What are you settling for in your life? What is so normal or average
that you just can't stand it anymore? It could be that you are settling
for a mediocre marriage, average grades in school, a normal routine
that has become nothing but a rut, a financial situation that has you
overwhelmed, and even spiritual complacency. When you take the
time to think about what it is, then it's time to ask yourself why.
Why are you content to be normal, average, or mediocre in any area
of your life? If you are ready for the extraordinary, then it is time to
step it up and expect more from yourself and the world around you.
The Bible says you have not because you ask not. So, what are you
asking for? Know what is best and accept nothing less.

65

"Then the same day at evening, being the first day of the
week, when the doors were shut where the disciples were
assembled for fear of the Jews, came Jesus and stood in the
midst of them, and saith unto them, Peace be unto you."
—John 20:19

ଔଔଔଔଔଔଔଔଔଔଔ

Let's take a few minutes to go back in time. For on this special
Easter Sunday many years ago, Jesus' disciples weren't celebrating at
all. They may have awakened with a sense of dread,
disappointment, and disillusionment. They had been serving Jesus
for over 3 years now and to watch him die such a horrific death on
the cross must have truly been the stuff that nightmares are made
of. What would they do now? Where would they go? They must
have felt so lost. That evening, when Jesus appeared to his disciples
for the first time, his words were words of peace. He was offering a
peace that passes all understanding. Are you feeling lost today? Go
to church and hear more about God's peace.

_____

_____

_____

_____

_____

66

"One of the most lasting pleasures you can experience is the feeling that comes over you when you genuinely forgive an enemy—whether he knows it or not."
—O. A. Battista

ଔଔଔଔଔଔଔଔଔଔଔ

Do you want more joy, more peace, and more pleasure in your life? If you do, then you will need to have plenty of room in your heart for forgiveness. According to the dictionary, forgiveness means that you cease to feel resentful towards another. In other words, you are no longer annoyed by the other person or hold ill will. Being in their presence does not make the hair on the back of your neck stand up or cause a ball in the pit of your stomach. You can wish them well in whatever direction they choose to go in their life. It means you are able to move on with your life, too. Is there someone in your life that you need to forgive? Take great pleasure in your day today, and forgive someone—whether they deserve it or not.

67

"God asks no man whether he will accept life. That is not
the choice. One must take it. The only choice is how."
—Henry Ward Beecher

C3 C3 C3 C3 C3 C3 C3 C3 C3 C3 C3

The fact that we have life and have been born into this world is
truly a gift, but sometimes life does not always give us what we
think we want or even deserve. No one wants to have a disease or a
disability, but sometimes life gives it to us. No one would choose to
have abusive parents, but some do. While we may not always agree
with it, if we are to grow and be the best that we can be, we must
accept where we are and what we have been given—the good and
the bad. Does it mean then that you give up, surrender, and turn
away in defeat? Not at all. Having an attitude of acceptance is a
simple peacefulness that rests in knowing that life is absolutely
perfect no matter what. Accept what is, not what you wish it were.

_____

_____

_____

_____

_____

68

"Advice is what we ask for when we know the answer but
wish we didn't."
—Erica Jong

෪෪෪෪෪෪෪෪෪෪෪

Isn't it true that when we are facing a problem we seek out advice
not because we don't know the right thing to do necessarily, but
mostly because we just don't want to do it, so, we look for other
options? While I am not saying that asking for advice is a bad
thing, I think sometimes we seek out advice as a means of escape. If
we follow someone else's advice and something goes wrong, it is
her fault, not ours. If we follow an alternate route, we can claim
ignorance and confusion from so many other opinions. When we
listen to our own intuition, our own still, small voice, we enter into
the role of taking responsibility for our own decisions. My advice—
take your own advice.

_____

_____

_____

_____

_____

69

"Learn to say no. It will be of more use to you than to be able to read Latin."

—Charles Haddon Spurgeon

C3 C3 C3 C3 C3 C3 C3 C3 C3 C3 C3

Did you know that you as an American citizen, as a responsible adult, and as a good parent have the option to say no? We know it is true, so why is it so difficult? It is difficult because we expect that when we say no someone else will get hurt by our saying it. After all, if we were the one doing the asking, we would be hurt—right? Maybe, maybe not. The answer to that depends on our inner thoughts and expectations for whether or not we thought they should say yes. Give up the idea that you know what others should say or do, and you will free yourself from the hurt of receiving a no. Communicate that this is not what you should do to the asker, and you will begin to learn to say no without guilt.

_____

_____

_____

_____

_____

70

"Expect people to be better than they are; it helps them to become better. But don't be disappointed when they are not; it helps them to keep trying."

—Merry Browne

ଔଔଔଔଔଔଔଔଔଔଔଔ

When a little one begins the exciting journey of taking his first steps, most parents will cheer, clap, get out the camcorder and save it forever in history. With those beginning steps, we expect that every day he will get a little more stable, a little bit more confident and a little bit faster. Will he have some run-ins with a few coffee tables that result in bumps and bruises? Sure, we expect that, too. And because we expect it, we aren't the least bit disappointed that he isn't ready for the Olympic tryouts yet. We understand where he is in his life, accept it, expect him to reach for more, and give him the room to fail as well as succeed. Expect people to be better while making room for them not to be.

_____

_____

_____

_____

_____

71

"There are no secrets to success. It is the result of
preparation, hard work, learning from failure."
—Gen. Colin L. Powell

C365365365365365365365365

Those that are successful know that they need to be prepared. So,
are you prepared? You may think so, but a better question just
might be—prepared for what? Successful people are prepared for
many things that you might not have given much thought to. For
example, successful people are prepared to drive a car by having car
insurance that will protect them from loss in the event of an
accident. Successful people prepare to earn more money by
managing what they already have. Successful people are prepared to
die by having a valid and current will that will protect their assets
and ensure they are given to those they choose. Be successful by
always being prepared for everything.

_____

_____

_____

_____

_____

72

"Nothing is really lost. It's just where it doesn't belong."
—Suzanne Mueller

ಂಚಂಚಂಚಂಚಂಚಂಚಂಚಂಚ

There have been moments in my household when I think that I am going insane. I look in my purse, on the table, under the bed, and in the closet knowing that I just left my keys in plain view on the kitchen counter, and now, they are gone. Somehow, as if by magic, the keys have run away, and I begin to wonder about myself. Losing things can be frustrating, time consuming, and stressful. If you find yourself in this situation often, then it is time to set up some orderliness for where things do belong. Pick one physical area in your life that needs to be put in order and get it back together. It could be your desk, your car, your closet, or your bedroom. Put some order back in your life.

_____

_____

_____

_____

_____

73

"It is better to debate a question without settling it than to settle a question without debating it."
—Joseph Joubert

ଔଔଔଔଔଔଔଔଔଔଔ

Think back for a minute to your inquisitive days of long ago when you were sitting in a classroom asking a lot of questions. Like most kids, we probably asked everything from "Why is the sky blue?" to "How do I solve this mathematical equation?" We asked everyone we knew from teachers, parents, neighbors, and friends. We may have even asked our inner selves questions about who we were and what would be our purpose in life. After all, there was so much to learn and we wanted to know it all. Then somewhere along our journey we stopped asking so many questions. Maybe we felt that we already knew all the answers. Challenge yourself to begin asking questions again. Do not just blindly accept what is told, but challenge, think, and reason it out. What if you don't know it all? Question everything.

_____

_____

_____

_____

_____

74

"If you play to win, as I do, the game never ends."
—Stan Mikita

છ્જ્છ્જ્છ્જ્છ્જ્છ્જ્છ્જ્

In this game of life, are you playing to win? You may think that winning the game of life will only come after years of struggle, sacrifice, and paying your dues, but what if you said you just want to win today. What if you could win every day? How would you play? Those that play the game of today and play to win have daily goals. Their daily goals are bite-sized so they will not overwhelm, yet significant enough to make a difference. They know the rules of the game and play within them so the thrill of winning is real—no cheating. They look forward to the game each day as they always have a gameplan and are excited to see how the plays will work out at the end of the day. Congratulations for being in the game. Play to win today.

_____

_____

_____

_____

_____

75

"Better is a dinner of herbs where love is, than a stalled ox
and hatred therewith."
—Proverbs 15:17

ରେ ରେ ରେ ରେ ରେ ରେ ରେ ରେ ରେ ରେ ରେ

What do you have on the dinner menu for today? Maybe you will
have a grilled steak with sautéed mushrooms and onions, a sweet
potato with butter and cinnamon, vegetables, and a salad with
cheesecake for dessert. Sounds wonderful! But as good as this meal
may sound to you, would you prefer to eat it with someone you
love or someone who is on your nerves because you just fought
over money? It would be better to eat macaroni and cheese for a
month than fight over money issues that have been created by
charging the expensive steaks. The best of meals, the best of houses,
and the best of things cannot be exchanged for love and harmony
within your home. Don't get confused by thinking that money can
buy love—either on cash or credit.

76

"One isn't born one's self. One is born with a mass of expectations, a mass of other people's ideas—and you have to work through it all."

—V. S. Naipaul

ભાભાભાભાભાભાભાભાભાભા

What is it that other people expect from you? From the time that we are born, our parents have expected each one of us to be geniuses, discover the cure for cancer, and become major league baseball players. When we go to school, our teachers expect us to excel in reading, writing, and arithmetic. When we go to college, we expect much from ourselves in being self-disciplined, getting our projects done on time and to the best of our ability. When we begin work, our boss expects us to be on time, be a quick learner, and say yes to every request. When we enter into marriage, we expect that our spouses will be perfect and we will have it all with kids, money, and a big house. Maybe it's time to let go of some of the expectations, and be grateful for what is.

_____

_____

_____

_____

_____

77

"The way to gain a good reputation is to endeavor to be what you desire to appear."
—Socrates

෯෯෯෯෯෯෯෯෯෯෯෯

Who do you appear to be? A person who is together, organized, peaceful, happy, wealthy, wise? These are all very good things and we would all like to be these, but are you really or are you just trying to convince everyone that you are something that you aren't? Becoming an actor, a hypocrite, a person who puts on the disguise is a tough role to play, but being found out for the truth might ruin your reputation—right? The trouble with that philosophy is that your pride is getting in the way of you really having all of those things you desire. If you aren't together and organized, consider a professional organizer. If you aren't happy and peaceful, talk with a counselor or coach to figure out why. Be what you appear to be.

_____

_____

_____

_____

_____

78

"The first sign of maturity is the discovery that the volume knob also turns to the left."
—"Smile" Zingers in Chicago Tribune

അജ്ഞാനജ്ഞാനജ്ഞാനജ്ഞാനജ്ഞാനജ്ഞാന

How many of you remember the days (or maybe you are still living the days) when your parents continually shouted, "Turn the music down!" It's a phase we all go through because we enjoy the music and we simply enjoy living out loud. But then there usually comes a time when we learn on our own to turn down the volume not because we have to, but because we want to. We want to because it is a sign of consideration for those around us. Does it mean that we are any less of an individual, stifling our creativity, or giving in to the masses? Not at all. It is an indication of maturity in that we appreciate those around us and are willing to be considerate of their needs. Live out loud, but do so with consideration.

_____

_____

_____

_____

_____

79

"Maturity begins when we're content to feel we're right about something without feeling the necessity to prove someone else wrong."

—Sydney J. Harris

ങ്ങങ്ങങ്ങങ്ങങ്ങങ്ങ

Have you ever watched an elderly couple who are engaged in a heated conversation over what they had for dinner last week at the local diner? Gertrude insists that they had the liver and onions because she remembers the smell of them as they were served to her by Gladys, the sister of Aunt Roberta's cousin. But Harold sends out a resounding note of irritation as he distinctly recalls having the spaghetti with meat sauce because he dripped some of the sauce on his tie. How many times do we find ourselves in battle over things that really have no meaning? Does it really matter what they ate last week? But even more importantly, does it really matter who is right? When it really doesn't matter, be right quietly.

_____

_____

_____

_____

_____

80

"There is no pillow so soft as a clear conscience."
—French Proverb

ఆఆఆఆఆఆఆఆఆఆఆ

How did you sleep last night? Did you toss and turn with the weight of the day on your shoulders and all the things that you feel you should have done the day before mixed in with the anxiety of all the things you should do tomorrow? We lay our heads down at night and our minds begin to spin with the voices reprimanding us for how inadequate we are, how lazy we've been, or how we'll never measure up. Our conscience fills with guilt and we dread the coming day. The challenge for you today is to eliminate at least 5 things that you feel you should do today so you can make room for more of what you want. Just cross them off the to-do list, and make other arrangements. Would you sleep better if you accomplished all that you truly wanted to do today? Live well today so you can sleep well tonight.

_____

_____

_____

_____

_____

81

"I don't know what the big deal is about old age. Old people who shine from the inside look 10 to 20 years younger."
—Dolly Parton

ରେ ରେ ରେ ରେ ରେ ରେ ରେ ରେ ରେ ରେ ରେ

Are you feeling a little old today? A little worn down, achy, sluggish, and not much energy to face the day. Then it is time to look at yourself in the mirror and smile. Just smile. People who naturally smile are people who naturally shine. There is a joy inside that is just waiting to come out, and sometimes if we just take a minute to smile at our own reflection, our inner selves will rise to the occasion and smile right back. If you are in the mood, you can even talk to yourself in the mirror and call the best of you to come out of hiding. Aging with all of its wrinkles, gray hair, and a little slower step cannot overpower your inner strength to shine. No matter how old you are—shine today.

82

"The most important thing a father can do for his children is to love their mother."
—Theodore Hesburgh

ରେ ରେ ରେ ରେ ରେ ରେ ରେ ରେ ରେ ରେ ରେ

Do you consider yourself one of the blessed ones in that you have a strong, loving family? Families are the single most important entity in raising strong individuals, strong leaders, strong communities, and a strong America. The quote above reminds a father that he needs to show his children that he loves their mother. How can you do this successfully? Begin with openly loving and showing affection for your wife in front of your children. Hugs and kisses for one another provide security and an example for how they will love their spouses someday. Ignore the moans and yucks that may come from the kids and enjoy the moments while teaching the very important life lessons. Give Mom a big kiss today.

_____

_____

_____

_____

_____

83

"The great gift of family is to be intimately acquainted with people you might never even introduce yourself to, had life not done it for you."

—Kendall Hailey

೫೫೫೫೫೫೫೫೫೫೫

Have you ever heard the simple expression—you can choose your friends, but you can't choose your family? One day you were just born into this world with a family. Nobody asked you which family you would like to have, which one would best prepare you for your calling, or which one would love you the way you want to be loved. God decided all of this for you. So while your parents may drive you nuts, the sibling rivalry sometimes gets the best of you, and Great Aunt Matilda just can't keep her nose out of things, these are the people that God has chosen to introduce you to. Every family is diverse, abnormal, and special. Be thankful for the family that God has given to you.

_____

_____

_____

_____

_____

84

"My father didn't tell me how to live; he lived, and let me watch him do it."
—Clarence Budington Kelland

છ્યાજાજાજાજાજાજાજાજાજાજા

Fathers and mothers, are you living a life that is a shining example of how to live? Would you be happy for your children if they chose to follow in your footsteps and live a life very similar to yours? Is your marriage so wonderful that you would hope that your children could be as happy as you someday? Is your career something that gives you joy and satisfaction and you would want for your children to have when they are ready? If any of these questions made you stop and say within yourself no, then it is time to begin living. It is time to have some fun, change your attitude, make some decisions, and grow into the person that you would want to see your children become. Be the example, and let them watch you live.

_____

_____

_____

_____

_____

85

"The word no carries a lot more meaning when spoken by a parent who also knows how to say yes."
—Joyce Maynard

CBCBCBCBCBCBCBCBCBCB

It's a really tough job being a parent and knowing when to say yes and when to say no can be a tough call. It seems that kids are always asking for something—candy, money, kool-aid, chips, and new toys. And there are days when I feel like all I've said all day is no. But what the children don't understand is that with every no is a yes. We say no to candy before dinner because we are saying yes to the nourishing of our children's bodies with good food. We say no to constant money requests because we say yes to the handling of money responsibly. And when we do have the opportunity to actually say yes, how sweet it is! Say yes to everything that is wonderful even when it is sometimes a no.

_____

_____

_____

_____

_____

86

"Chains do not hold a marriage together. It is threads, hundreds of tiny threads, which sew people together through the years."
—Simone Signoret

ೞೞೞೞೞೞೞೞೞೞೞ

There is a story about a little boy who was watching his mother cross-stitching a blanket. It was a big blanket so the mother worked on it whenever she could. The little boy was very little and couldn't see what his mother was doing, but could only see the messy threads from underneath. He looked at all the colors from below and decided he only liked the bright ones. He didn't understand that the dark threads define, add depth, and actually bring the picture to life. So it is with us. Sometimes we don't understand the mess and the dark threads from down here below, but God does. He knows just the perfect threads to make a beautiful picture of marriage, family, and life. Give up the ball and chain and pick up a needle and thread.

_____

_____

_____

_____

_____

87

"Human beings, by changing the inner attitude of their minds, can change the outer aspect of their lives."
—William James

ርቼርቼርቼርቼርቼርቼርቼርቼርቼርቼ

So how does one go about changing the inner attitude of his mind? We know that attitude is so important because it shades and colors all that we see around us. Depending on our attitude, we can see a challenge as a fun, exciting event that we have the strength and determination to overcome, or we can see that same challenge as insurmountable and not even worth giving it a try for it will beat us anyway. It's all about attitude. If you want to begin changing that inner attitude, try this. Get a rubberband to have around your wrist and everytime you have a doubt, a gripe, or a bad attitude snap it. The idea is to change the pattern that you have developed within yourself. No pain, no gain.

_____

_____

_____

_____

_____

88

"He which soweth sparingly shall reap also sparingly; and he which soweth bountifully shall reap also bountifully."
—II Corinthians 9:6

ଔଔଔଔଔଔଔଔଔଔଔ

Do you want more abundance in your life? Not only abundance of wealth, although there is nothing wrong with that, but also an abundance of love, talent, attention, compliments, wisdom, smiles, time, and whatever else comes to your mind. The Bible gives us this clear picture of how to make that happen. Whatever it is that you want more of, give what you have of that away to someone else. It sounds so contradictory to think that we could actually have more by giving it away instead of hoarding, stashing, and keeping it all to ourselves, but it is nevertheless true. Challenge yourself to give away something that is precious to you and you would like more of. See if it doesn't come back to you a hundredfold. Givers get.

_____
_____
_____
_____
_____

89

"If a man happens to find himself, he has a mansion which he can inhabit with dignity all the days of his life."
—James A. Michener

ŒŒŒŒŒŒŒŒŒŒŒŒ

What is your net worth? According to a balance sheet, the way to figure this out is to add all of your assets, subtract all of your liabilities from that, and then you have your net worth. It can be quite an eye opener to do this, and while it is important to do, it really is not a true picture of your actual worth. There are many things that do not show up in the numbers, and yet we know they are valuable assets nonetheless. Things like courage, determination, integrity, creativity, selling skills, and even time management abilities. These are your "invisible assets", and while these may not show up on a balance sheet, they are of great value. Use all of your "invisible assets" today to increase your net worth.

90

"Be honorable yourself if you wish to associate with
honorable people."
—Welsh Proverb

○₃○₃○₃○₃○₃○₃○₃○₃○₃○₃○₃

How would you describe some of your closest friends? Are they
happy, creative, and honorable or are they miserable, complainers,
and liars? Why do I ask this? Because whether we like it or not, we
become like those that we associate with. If you want to be happier,
then maybe it's time to hang around others who are happy. Want to
be more creative, find some other creative people and spend some
time with them. Want to have more fun, associate with those that
know how to have fun and not regret it in the morning. You have
the power to choose who you want to be simply by making great
choices about who you associate with. Choose your friends wisely.

_____

_____

_____

_____

_____

91

"To keep a lamp burning, we have to keep putting oil in it."
—Mother Teresa

જાજાજાજાજાજાજાજાજાજા

How is your light shining these days? Is it burning brightly and glowing with the joy of life or are you burning too much midnight oil and your light is almost nonexistent? If you find the latter to be true, then it is time to put some more oil into your lamp. So, where does the oil for your lamp come from? It comes from taking care of yourself, and you know what fuels you best. Maybe it's exercising, a massage, a good book, a great night out with friends, a weekend away with your special someone, going to church. A lamp that doesn't have any oil cannot do what it was designed to do, and neither can you. May your motto today be—This little light of mine, I'm gonna let it shine.

_____

_____

_____

_____

_____

92

"Happiness is when what you think, what you say, and what you do are in harmony."
—Gandhi

03030303030303030303

While all of you reading this thought may not be able to sing in harmony, most of us know it when we hear it. It is the beautiful sound of an orchestra playing a Brahm's lullaby that soothes the soul and renews the spirit. It is a duet or trio singing an old gospel tune that encourages us to clap and shout with joy. And it is when all that we think, say, and do is in harmony that we are truly happy. Life begins to get out of tune and becomes unhappy when we make decisions that are not in line with what we believe and value. If you value truth, do not lie. If you love your family, spend precious time with them. If you believe in your marriage vows, be faithful to them. Live in the happiness of harmony.

_____

_____

_____

_____

_____

93

"My motto was to keep swinging. Whether I was in a slump or feeling badly or having trouble off the field, the only thing to do was to keep swinging."

—Hank Aaron

ಚಿಚಿಚಿಚಿಚಿಚಿಚಿಚಿಚಿಚಿಚಿ

Do you have a purpose? Do you have a simple way of looking at life that is a mission statement for how you choose to live it? For Hank Aaron, his mission, his motto, was to keep swinging. It didn't matter how he felt, what was going on around him, or what obstacles were in his way, his goal, his purpose, his desire was just to keep on swinging. It's simple. Sometimes we get our lives so complicated and overloaded with detailed explanations of what we feel we need to do or who we need to be. What if instead we determined to simply keep on loving? No matter what came our way, we would love anyway. What if we purposed to trust? Trust in the hard times and the good times. Keep your mission, your purpose, your goal simple.

_____

_____

_____

_____

_____

94

"I know that I'm never as good or bad as any single performance. I've never believed my critics or my worshippers, and I've always been able to leave the game at the arena."
—Charles Barkley

 C3C3C3C3C3C3C3C3C3C3C3C3

Everyday gives us new opportunities to perform. To do whatever it is that we are designed to do. Maybe your performance is on the job, in front of an audience, in front of your family, or in front of the mirror, but we all have the opportunity to do something that is unique and wonderful. The key is to know that no one performance whether it is our best or our worst determines the value of who we are. When you close your eyes at the end of the day today, you may be proud of your performance or you may replay every move with regret, but when the day is done it's time to leave the game at the arena and move on. Tomorrow gives us another opportunity to play again. Your life is bigger than any one achievement or any one mistake.

_____

_____

_____

_____

_____

95

"Rudeness is the weak man's imitation of strength."
—Eric Hoffer

CBCBCBCBCBCBCBCBCBCB

Have you ever found yourself so at the end of your rope that you blurted out something that you knew was very rude, but said it anyway? In the moment, it may have given you a false sense of strength that you were brave enough to finally say what you had to say no matter what the consequences. But later, you wonder why you said it, and regret hurting someone else even if they were rude first. What's the solution? Say what needs to be said before you reach the end of your rope. Sometimes we get concerned that if we tell someone the truth it will sound rude, but there is always a way to speak the truth in love and grace. Be strong enough to speak without rudeness.

_____

_____

_____

_____

_____

96

"Anyone can make the easy choice—something bad for something good—but very few people have the insight and courage to make the tough choice of letting go of good things in order to have better things."
—Lloyd Campbell

೫೮೫೮೫೮೫೮೫೮೫೮೫೮೫೮

Life is always changing, and new things are always coming into our lives. Sometimes our lives get too full with all these new things and we need to make some tough decisions as to what needs to go and what gets to stay. Making a choice between good and bad isn't so bad, but deciding between what is good and what is better can be a lot more challenging. It takes a lot of courage to say no to tennis lessons for little Susie when Mom and Dad are working hard at getting out of debt. It may take sacrifice to let go of a second income for a child to have a parent at home. It takes dedication to go to church instead of enjoying a day on the golf course. Have the courage to let go of the good things in order to have the better things.

_____

_____

_____

_____

_____

97

"Reflect upon your present blessings, of which every man has many—not on your past misfortunes, of which all men have some."

—Charles Dickens

ﷲﷲﷲﷲﷲﷲﷲﷲﷲﷲ

Let's take a few minutes today and reflect on the many blessings of which we all have many. Let's celebrate the weather whether if be sunshine or rain. Let's be thankful for our families whether they are near of far away. Let's be grateful for our minds which are able to read, comprehend, and learn. Let's enjoy the breath of life that is given to us by God each day. No matter where you are or what you are facing today, there is always something to be thankful for. And while all of us have some misfortunes in our past, we can choose not to dwell there, but rather choose to reflect upon the blessings that are here for us to notice today. Count your many blessings, name them one by one.

_____

_____

_____

_____

_____

98

"Our prayers are answered not when we are given what we ask, but when we are challenged to be what we can be."
—Morris Adler

ଔଔଔଔଔଔଔଔଔଔଔ

Just recently, I was challenged with this question—What is the point of our lives? Is the point to be happy all the time? Is the purpose for us to all be wealthy, famous, or successful? Is it to go from one accomplishment to the next? So, what is the point? For me, the point is for God Himself to bring into my life the things that will mold me and shape me into an image that is pleasing to Him. My response to the Potter's hands may be happiness or sadness, but both of those are perfectly okay as long as I am open to the greater purpose. It's when I try to be something that I am not or judge myself on how I am feeling that I miss the point. Are you getting the point yet?

_____

_____

_____

_____

_____

99

"One of the nicest things about life is the way we must regularly stop whatever it is we are doing and devote our attention to eating."

—Luciano Pavarotti

ભ ભ ભ ભ ભ ભ ભ ભ ભ ભ ભ

How wonderfully true this quote is! Not a day goes by that is not interrupted by moments of eating at one time or another. Sometimes those moments are hurried while driving through a drive-through. Others are moments of laughter and conversation around the dinner table with family. Occasionally, they are nights out at our favorite restaurant with friends. Eating is a necessity in which all of us must take part. Without eating, we would whither up and die. So, if this is a major part of our daily lives, why not enjoy it? Why not take each bite, whether fat free or not, as an opportunity to enjoy every part of our life even if it is as simple and normal as eating. You are what you eat, so enjoy it.

_____

_____

_____

_____

_____

100

"The finest fruit of serious learning should be the ability to speak the word God without reserve or embarrassment."
—Nathan M. Pusey

ଔଔଔଔଔଔଔଔଔଔଔଔ

In this part of the Midwest, it is not uncommon for people to end a conversation with "God bless you!" On our money, we see the phrase "In God we trust". In our pledge of allegiance, we say "One nation under God". God is a part of our culture, our way of life. But how do you feel when you say the word God? Does it feel strange, and in the moment you wonder if it was an appropriate time to mention Him? By simply mentioning the name of God, you are sharing with the world your belief system, your spirituality, the most precious side of you. My challenge for you today is to begin to discover and dig deeper into your spirituality for it is a major part of who you are. God bless your body, soul, and spirit today.

_____

_____

_____

_____

_____

A Quick Afterthought...

If you've just completed your 100 days, I want to be the first to congratulate you because I doubt there is anyone else who will!! Reading through this book a day at a time, and thinking through new and different ideas is a private and intimate journey. Let me encourage you to take another 90 seconds and be very proud of yourself!

As you set this book aside for now, I hope that you will come back to it often to review your favorites. For me, I hope that this is just the beginning and more of these books will be following shortly.

Thank you for having spent this time with me, and if there is something you'd like to share about your journey, I'd love to hear from you. Feel free to e-mail me at <u>Gloria@GloriaCoach.com</u>.

With love,

Gloria

About the Author:

Gloria Swardenski, also know as Gloria Coach, is an internationally known Life and Business Coach, Newspaper Columnist, and Professional Speaker. As a coach, she works with clients from around the world on issues ranging from professional business management for entrepreneurs and corporations to balancing work and family life while achieving personal and professional goals.

As a business owner herself, Gloria is in the trenches concerning what leaders in organizations and businesses face in regard to changing business climates, personnel issues and the importance of consistency in excellent customer service. As a former corporate CEO and an entrepreneur with a company just months away from nationally franchising, she brings cutting edge insight for leaders and those who make the difference in the day to day operations of a business.

Gloria is also a wife and mother to four beautiful and brilliant young children. In this, her most challenging role, she understands the need for powerful 90 second time slots and the challenge of keeping our minds and attitudes sharp when the laundry piles are a bit overwhelming.

To learn more about Gloria or inquire about an upcoming speaking event, visit www.GloriaCoach.com.

Index by Quote Reference:

0-595-32274-3